MEET DOROTHEA LANGE

Read With You
Center for Excellence in STEAM Education

Read With You

Published by Read With You Publishing. Printed in the United States of America.

ISBN: 979-8-88618-499-0
First Edition: September 2023

I am Dorothea Lange, an American documentary photographer. That means I try to photograph life as it really is. This is my most famous photo.

People call it "Migrant Mother." Why might this photo be so powerful? And what is a *migrant*?

Migrant Mother, 1936

A *migrant* is a person who leaves home to move to another place. Have you ever moved somewhere new?

During the Great Depression, I took many pictures of the people who had to leave their homes to look for work.

Children of Migratory Carrot Pullers, Mexicans.
Imperial Valley, California, 1937

My photos show the lives of people in difficult times. Imagine the stories this grandmother might tell.

Many people were hungry and couldn't find work in her home state of Oklahoma, so she came to California for a new life.

Grandmother from Oklahoma and Her Pieced Quilt.
California, Kern County, 1936

I was born in New Jersey, but I moved to sunny California. I hoped my pictures would show people's struggles and make the world better.

I wanted my photos to give dignity and power to people who were facing hardship.

Filipino Boy of a Labor Gang Cutting Cauliflower near Santa Maria, California, 1937

The small details also tell a story.
What machine might this be,
hiding in the background?

Check the plaque. What is the woman's job? Do you think it would be easy work or hard work?

Cotton Picker. Southern San Joaquin Valley, California, 1936

My most famous pictures are from the Great Depression, but I also photographed a sad time for people of Japanese descent in America.

During World War II, they were forced to leave their homes because Japan had attacked America, although these people were not a part of the attack.

Evacuees of Japanese Ancestry Lining Up before Japanese-American Citizens League to Register Prior to Their Evacuation and Going to War Relocation Authority Centers for the Duration of the War, 1942

No one should be forced out of their home. My photographs show the people hurt by the government's decisions.

Even though the United States paid me to take pictures, I bravely spoke up when I disagreed with the government's decisions.

Manzanar, Calif. June 1942. Kinu Hirashima, from Los Angeles, Perching in an Apple Tree at Manzanar, War Relocation Authority Center Where the Evacuees of Japanese Ancestry Will Spend the Duration of the War, 1942

If you document injustice with your camera, maybe you can change the world, too!

To Harvest the Crops of California Thousands of Families Live Literally on Wheels, San Joaquin Valley, 1935

Find Examples

This photograph is *Waiting for the Semimonthly Relief Checks at Calipatria, Imperial Valley, California* (1937).

What does the title tell us about this photo? Ask an adult if you are not sure.

Fifteen years before this photo was taken, these men owned their own farms. How do you think they felt during the Great Depression?

Find another photo in the book with someone who is expressing similar feelings.

How can you tell that Lange respects the men she is photographing?

Connect

This photograph is *Toward Los Angeles, California* (1937).

Why did Lange photograph these men next to a sign about the train?

Why do you think the men in this picture are not taking the train?

How would you feel if you left your home and went to look for work somewhere else?

What is Lange saying about the Great Depression through this photo?

NEXT TIME TRY THE TRAIN
RELAX
Southern Pacific

Craft

Option 1

1. Ask someone who has lived a long time to tell you about a struggle they overcame.
2. Photograph them and turn the photo black and white, so it looks like Lange's photos.
3. Write a paragraph explaining why it is important to honor this person's life.

Option 2

1. Find something broken, like an abandoned house or crumbling wall.
2. Take a photo of it.
3. Share your photo with others and explain how this place could be made useful or beautiful again.

Explore fun facts about interesting painters by visiting
https://www.readwithyou.com/pages/meet-the-artist-activities